Celebrating Fathers

Celebrating Fathers

by

Teri Wilhelms

Rutledge Hill Press®
Nashville, Tennessee
A Thomas Nelson Company

Published by Rutledge Hill Press, a Thomas Nelson company, P.O. Box 141000, Nashville, Tennessee 37214.

Library of Congress Cataloging-in-Publication Data

ISBN: 1-55853-899-2

Printed in Colombia
1 2 3 4 5 6 7 8 9—06 05 04 03 02 01

Celebrating Fathers

A little child, a limber elf,
Singing, dancing to itself . . .
Makes such a vision to the sight
As fills a father's eyes with light.

SAMUEL TAYLOR COLERIDGE

*T*o bring up a child in a way he should go, travel that way yourself once in a while.

JOSH BILLINGS

—m—

*H*e that will have his son have respect for him and his orders, must himself have a great reverence for his son.

JOHN LOCKE

A baby has a way of making a man out of his father and a boy out of his grandfather.

ANGIE PAPADAKIS

*H*appy that man whose children make his happiness in life and not his grief.

EURIPIDES

I am determined that my children shall be brought up in their father's religion, if they can find out what it is.

CHARLES LAMB

*D*on't take up a man's time talking about the smartness of your children; he wants to talk to you about the smartness of his.

E. W. HOWE

*F*athers send their sons to college either because they went to college or because they didn't.

L. L. HENDERSON

—⸎—

*T*he best thing a father can do for a son is give him forty pounds and throw him out the door.

W. SOMERSET MAUGHAM

I was never more pleased with my son than on the day he saw a John Wayne western on TV and told me I could have handled those rustlers just as well.

EVAN MCNAUGHTON

*M*anual labor to my father was not only good and decent for its own sake, but as he was given to saying, it straightened out one's thoughts.

MARY ELLEN CHASE

*D*irectly after God in heaven comes Papa.

WOLFGANG AMADEUS MOZART

*M*y earliest recollections are of being dressed up and allowed to come down to dance for a group of gentlemen who applauded and laughed as I pirouetted before them. Finally, my father would pick me up and hold me high in the air. He dominated my life as long as he lived, and was the love of my life for many years after he died.

ELEANOR ROOSEVELT

I don't know who my grandfather was; I'm much more concerned to know what his grandson will be.

ABRAHAM LINCOLN

—ᴍ—

*L*ive so that your son, when people tell him that he reminds them of you, will stick out his chest, not his tongue.

THE FURROW

*T*he best thing to give to your enemy is forgiveness; to an opponent, tolerance; to a friend, your heart; to your child, a good example; to a father, deference; to your mother, conduct that will make her proud of you; to yourself, respect; to all men, charity.

FRANCIS MAITLAND BALFOUR

*M*y father used to say, "Let them see you and not the suit. That should be secondary."

CARY GRANT

—⚊—

*H*appy is he that is happy in his children.

THOMAS FULLER

*Y*ou've got to do your own growing, no matter how tall your grandfather was.

IRISH PROVERB

*I*t is not the rich man you should properly call happy, but him who knows how to use with wisdom the blessings of the gods, to endure hard poverty, and who fears dishonor worse than death, and is not afraid to die for cherished friends or fatherland.

HORACE

*P*arenthood isn't a picnic. Dad may work from sunup to sundown, but as a father he's never done.

WILLIAM D. WILKINS

—∭—

*F*or rarely are sons similar to their fathers: most are worse, and a few are better than their fathers.

HOMER

*S*how me who your parents are and I'll show you who once paid for your diapers.

HARRIET TELEMAN

—⚬—

A man finds out what is meant by a spitting image when he tries to feed cereal to his infant.

IMOGENE FEY

*E*verybody knows that fatherhood reveals your limitations. But less well known is that, now and then, fatherhood also brings out skills that might well have gone undiscovered were it not for having kids.

HUGH O'NEILL

A child enters your home and for the next twenty years makes so much noise you can hardly stand it. The child departs, leaving the house so silent you think you are going mad.

JOHN ANDREW HOLMES

—⧈—

*H*e may be president, but he still comes home and swipes my socks.

JOSEPH P. KENNEDY, TALKING ABOUT HIS SON JOHN

All we have of freedom—all we use or know—
This our fathers bought for us, long, long ago.

RUDYARD KIPLING

Nothing feebler than a man does the earth raise up, of all the things which breathe and move on the earth, for he believes that he will never suffer evil in the future, as long as the gods give him success and he flourishes in his strength; but when the blessed gods bring sorrows too to pass, even these he bears, against his will, with steadfast spirit, for the thoughts of earthly men are like the day which the father of gods and men brings upon them.

HOMER

The place of the father in the modern suburban family is a very small one, particularly if he plays golf.

BERTRAND RUSSELL

—⁂—

Education is something you get when your father sends you to college. But it isn't complete until you send your son there.

UNKNOWN

*N*o one would be foolish enough to choose war over peace—in peace sons bury their fathers, but in war fathers bury their sons.

CROESUS OF LYDIA

Children's children are the crown of old men, and
the glory of children is their father.

PROVERBS 17:6

—〜〜—

If a man leaves little children behind him, it is as if
he did not die.

MOROCCAN PROVERB

*I*f you look up "Intelligence" in the new volumes of the *Encyclopedia Britannica*, you'll find it classified under the following three heads: Intelligence, Human; Intelligence, Animal; Intelligence, Military. My stepfather's a perfect specimen of Intelligence, Military.

ALDOUS HUXLEY

*A*gain, men in general desire the good, and not merely what their fathers had.

ARISTOTLE

—⁓—

*M*y father was not a failure. After all he was the father of a president of the United States.

HARRY S. TRUMAN

*C*hildren are poor men's riches.

THOMAS FULLER

—ɯ—

*F*ather's Day is like Mother's Day, except the gift is cheaper.

GERALD F. LIEBERMAN

*P*arenthood is uncertainty. I always figure out what my kids need from me just as they no longer need it. If I can determine their position precisely, I miss how fast they're going. All the million moments of affection and impatience get mushed together.

HUGH O'NEILL

When I was a boy of fourteen, my father was so ignorant I could hardly stand to have the old man around. But when I got to be twenty-one, I was astonished at how much the old man had learned in seven years.

MARK TWAIN

*L*isten to your father, who gave you life.

PROVERBS 23:22

—ɷ—

A good name and good advice is all your dad can give you.

HARRY S. TRUMAN

I only realized it much later, but my father gave me a wonderful gift: a love of and joy in learning.

DR. RUTH WESTHEIMER

—◊◊—

*E*very word and deed of a parent is a fiber woven into the character of a child, which ultimately determines how that child fits into the fabric of society.

DAVID WILKERSON

*T*he words that a father speaks to
his children in the privacy of home
are not heard by the world, but, as in
whispering galleries, they are clearly
heard at the end, and by posterity.

JEAN PAUL RICHTER

I once complained to my father that I didn't seem to be able to do things the same way other people did. Dad's advice? "Margo, don't be a sheep. People hate sheep. They eat sheep."

MARGO KAUFMAN

*M*y father never raised his hand to any one of his children, except in self-defense.

FRED ALLEN

—〰—

*F*athers, provoke not your children to anger, lest they be discouraged.

COLOSSIANS 3:21

*T*o be a successful father there's one absolute rule: when you have a kid, don't look at it for the first two years.

ERNEST HEMINGWAY

———✠———

*M*others are fonder than fathers of their children because they are more certain they are their own.

ARISTOTLE

*M*y father and I had one of those English friendships which began by avoiding intimacies and eventually eliminated speech altogether.

JORGE LUIS BORGES

I watched a small man with thick calluses on both hands work fifteen and sixteen hours a day. I saw him once literally bleed from the bottoms of his feet, a man who came here uneducated, alone, unable to speak the language, who taught me all I needed to know about faith and hard work by the simple eloquence of his example.

MARIO CUOMO

*N*ot a tenth of us who are in business are doing as well as we could if we merely followed the principles that were known to our grandfathers.

WILLIAM FEATHER

—␣—

A father is someone who carries pictures where his money used to be.

LION

I grew up to have my father's looks—my father's speech patterns, my father's posture, my father's walk, my father's opinions—and my mother's contempt for my father.

JULES FEIFFER

—ᴠᴠ—

*S*he got her good looks from her father. He's a plastic surgeon.

GROUCHO MARX

*L*ife is all one piece. Men err when they think they can be inhuman exploiters in their business life, and loving husbands and fathers at home. For achievement without love is a cold and tight-lipped murderer of human happiness everywhere.

SMILEY BLANTON

He never cares to wander from his own fireside,
He never cares to wander or to roam,
With his baby on his knee,
He's as happy as can be,
For there's no place like home, sweet home.

FELIX MCGLENNON

*F*atherhood has been an occasion to stand near my son's flame and to witness the emergence of a moral man.

HUGH O'NEILL

—∞—

*W*hat you have inherited from your father, you must earn over again for yourselves, or it will not be yours.

JOHANN WOLFGANG VON GOETHE

The debt of gratitude we owe our mother and father goes forward, not backward. What we owe our parents is the bill presented to us by our children.

MARY ELLEN CHASE

*F*atherhood is pretending the present you love most is soap-on-a-rope.

BILL COSBY

—⟋⟍—

*I*f it were natural for fathers to care for their sons, they would not need so many laws commanding them to do so.

PHYLLIS CHESLER

No man is responsible for his father. That was entirely his mother's affair.

MARGARET TURNBULL

——∞——

My father hated radio and could not wait for television to be invented so he could hate that too.

PETER DE VRIES

*B*uried not-so-deep in the
subconscious of most fathers is an
idealized image of Dad the Teacher,
the man who passes on knowledge.

HUGH O'NEILL

*O*ne father is more than a hundred schoolmasters.

GEORGE HERBERT

—∿—

A father is always making his baby into a little woman. And when she is a woman he turns her back again.

ENID BAGNOLD

*T*he more people have studied different methods of bringing up children the more they have come to the conclusion that what good mothers and fathers instinctively feel like doing for their babies is the best after all.

BENJAMIN SPOCK

*B*abies don't need fathers, but mothers do. Someone who is taking care of a baby needs to be taken care of.

AMY HECKERLING

—⁂—

*T*here is never much trouble in any family where the children hope someday to resemble their parents.

WILLIAM LYON PHELPS

*T*here are three stages in a man's life:
"My Daddy can whip your Daddy."
"Aw, Dad, you don't know anything."
"My father used to say. . . ."

DWIGHT MCSMITH

*I*t is a wise father that knows his own child.

WILLIAM SHAKESPEARE

—⧢—

*T*he sins of the fathers are often visited upon the sons-in-law.

JOAN KISER

*H*e also emphasized that a man's dignity lives after him; it's what you contribute to this world that matters, not what you take out of it. The essence of love is not to be loved but to give love.

RICARDO MONTALBAN, SPEAKING OF HIS FATHER

*B*uying a stereo is merely a father's practice for the Big Buy: a car. When his child requests a car, a father will wish that he were a member of some sect that hasn't gone beyond the horse.

BILL COSBY

*Y*ou know, fathers just have a way of putting everything together.

ERICKA COSBY

—m—

*I*t's a wise child that knows its own father, and an unusual one who unreservedly approves of him.

MARK TWAIN

The father who does not teach his son his duties is equally guilty with the son who neglects them.

CONFUCIUS

—◊—

This is the duty of a father, to accustom his son to act rightly of his own accord than from unnatural fear.

TERENCE

*M*others give sons permission to be princes, but the fathers must show them how. . . . Fathers give daughters permission to be princesses, and mothers must show them how. Otherwise, both boys and girls will grow up and always see themselves as frogs.

ERIC BERNE

I've always followed my father's advice: he told me, first, to always keep my word and, second, to never insult anybody unintentionally. If I insult you, you can be damn sure I intend to. And, third, he told me not to go around looking for trouble.

JOHN WAYNE

A man knows when he is growing old because he begins to look like his father.

GABRIEL GARCÍA MÁRQUEZ

—⬩—

*T*he most important thing that parents can teach their children is how to get along without them.

FRANK A. CLARK

*B*ecoming a father is easy enough. But being one is rough.

WILHELM BUSCH

—m—

*M*any an excellent man is tempted to forget that the best offering he can make to his children is himself.

HENRY NEUMANN

Be kind to thy father,
For when thou were young,
Who loved thee so fondly as he?
He caught the first accents that fell from thy tongue,
And joined in thy innocent glee.

MARGARET COURTNEY

*M*y father had always said there are four things a child needs: plenty of love, nourishing food, regular sleep, and lots of soap and water. After that, what he needs most is some intelligent neglect.

IVY BAKER PRIEST

Blessed indeed is the man who hears many gentle voices call him father!

LYDIA M. CHILD

—ⱳ—

By the time a man realizes that maybe his father was right, he usually has a son who thinks he's wrong.

CHARLES WADSWORTH

*D*o not under any circumstances borrow money from your father if you're over the age of thirty-two. If you need parental cash and you're older than that, it had better be for a business investment in an office condo or something. If it's cash for groceries and bills, you're in bad shape if you ask the old man. But you're in worse shape if he says, "Sure." Delaying personal maturity is far more expensive than delaying maturity on a CD to avoid going to the First Bank of Dad.

DENIS BOYLES

*I*f there is a measure of good parenthood, it could be when our children exceed our own achievements.

TOM HAGGAI

—∿—

*D*iogenes struck the father when the son swore.

ROBERT BURTON

*M*y father must have had some elementary education for he could read and write and keep accounts inaccurately.

GEORGE BERNARD SHAW

—⚬—

*I*t behooves a father to be blameless if he expects his son to be.

HOMER

A father never feels worthy of the worship in a child's eyes. He's never quite the hero his daughter thinks he is, never quite the man his son believes him to be, and this worries him sometimes. So he works too hard to try and smooth the rough places in the road for those of his own who will follow him.

PAUL HARVEY

*I*t's only when you grow up and step back from him, or leave him for your own career and your own home—it's only then that you can measure his greatness and fully appreciate it. Pride reinforces love.

MARGARET TRUMAN

*L*ike father, like son.

PROVERB

—◊—

*W*hat was silent in the father speaks in the son; and often I found the son the unveiled secret of the father.

FRIEDRICH NIETZSCHE

*I*t's a wise father who knows as much as his own child.

JUDGE

—◊—

*B*y profession I am a soldier and take pride in that fact. But I am prouder, infinitely prouder, to be a father.

GENERAL DOUGLAS MACARTHUR

*M*y father didn't tell me how to live; he lived and let me watch him do it.

CLARENCE B. KELLAND

—⚏—

*W*e never know the love of the parent till we become parents ourselves.

HENRY WARD BEECHER

There are three ways to get something done: (1) Do it yourself. (2) Hire someone to do it for you. (3) Forbid your kids to do it.

UNKNOWN

*T*hat is the thankless position of the father in the family—the provider for all and the enemy of all.

J. AUGUST STRINDBERG

—⁂—

*M*y father always used to say that when you die, if you've got five real friends, you've had a great life.

LEE IACOCCA

*Y*ou don't raise heroes, you raise sons. If you treat them like sons, they'll turn out to be heroes, even if it's just in your own eyes.

WALTER SCHIRRA SR.

*H*e's given me the greatest treasure a father can give—a piece of himself.

SUZANNE CHAZIN

*H*is father watched him across the gulf of years and pathos which always must divide a father from his son.

JOHN MARQUAND

*I*f the new American father feels bewildered and even defeated, let him take comfort from the fact that whatever he does in any fathering situation has a fifty percent chance of being right.

BILL COSBY

A father is a banker provided by nature.

FRENCH PROVERB

—⟋⟍—

*T*he fundamental defect with fathers is that they want their children to be a credit to them.

BERTRAND RUSSELL

*T*he sooner you treat your son as a man, the sooner he will be one.

JOHN DRYDEN

—⬩⬩⬩—

*Y*ou don't have to deserve your mother's love. You have to deserve your father's. He's more particular.

ROBERT FROST

*I*f the relationship of father to son could really be reduced to biology, the whole earth would blaze with the glory of fathers and sons.

JAMES BALDWIN

*H*onor thy father and thy mother" stands written among the three laws of most revered righteousness.

AESCHYLUS

—⚋—

*I*f there is any immortality to be had among us human beings, it is certainly only in the love that we leave behind. Fathers like mine don't ever die.

LEO BUSCAGLIA

When all is said and done, fatherhood comes down to this. Be big. Be small. Be quiet. Make noise. Don't dance in front of your kids' friends. Save. Spend. Stay off the whirling ride of death. And love their mother.

HUGH O'NEILL

*J*oseph Lister, aged ten, was waiting for his father to inspect his lessons, when he happened to look out of the window. He was startled by a remarkable sight; owing to a defect in the glass, a kind of bubble had formed, and when he looked through the bubble he could see everything outside much more clearly than he could when he looked through the rest of the glass.

He asked his father for the explanation. His father told him that the bubble was acting as a magnifying glass, and could not explain it, but promised to look it up in a book of optics. This aroused Joseph's interest in optics. He was to invent the achromatic lens and to become a Fellow of the Royal Society.

R. S. & C. M. ILLINGWORTH

I cannot think of any need in childhood as strong as the need for a father's protection.

SIGMUND FREUD

———

*B*efore I got married I had six theories about bringing up children. Now I have six children and no theories.

JOHN WILMOT

*F*athers should not get too discouraged if their sons reject their advice. It will not be wasted; years later the sons will offer it to their own offspring.

UNKNOWN

An optimist is a father who lets his teen-age son take the car on a date. A pessimist is a father who will not. A cynic is a father who did.

LYNDON JOHNSON

*T*he child had every toy his father wanted.

ROBERT C. WHITTEN

—⚬—

A man never stands as tall as when he kneels to help a child.

KNIGHTS OF PYTHAGORAS

*I*t doesn't matter who my father was; it matters who I remember he was.

ANNE SEXTON

—⚏—

*F*ather's Day—When a man who is proud of his family finds his family is proud of him.

UNKNOWN

*H*ow pleasant it is for a father to sit at his child's board. It is like an aged man reclining under the shadow of an oak which he has planted.

WALTER SCOTT

Children aren't happy without something to ignore,
And that's what parents were created for.

OGDEN NASH

The best money advice ever given me was from my father. When I was a little girl, he told me, "Don't spend anything unless you have to."

DINAH SHORE

—⅏—

The mark of a good parent is that he can have fun while being one.

MARCELENE COX

*H*e who has daughters is always a Shepherd.

SPANISH PROVERB

—⚹—

I'll meet the raging of the skies, but not an angry father.

THOMAS CAMPBELL

*N*othing is dearer to a father than a daughter. Sons have spirits of higher pitch, but sons aren't given to showing affection.

EURIPIDES

*T*o be a good parent, you have to put yourself second, to recognize that the child has feelings and needs separate from yours, and fulfill those needs without expecting anything in return.

HOWARD KOGAN

*C*hildren are the living messages we send to a time we will not see.

JOHN W. WHITEHEAD

—⟋⟍—

*I*f you must hold yourself up to your children, hold yourself up as an object lesson and not as an example.

GEORGE BERNARD SHAW

*I*n a short story titled "The Capital of the World," Nobel Prize–winning author Ernest Hemingway tells about a father and a teenage son, Paco, whose relationship breaks down. After the son runs away from home, the father begins a long journey in search of him. Finally, as a last resort, the man puts an ad in the local newspaper in Madrid. It reads, "Dear Paco, meet me in front of the newspaper office tomorrow at noon . . . all is forgiven . . . I love you." The next morning, in front of the newspaper office were eight hundred men named Paco, desiring to restore broken relationships with their fathers.

The most important thing a father can do for his children is to love their mother.

HENRY WARD BEECHER

———

A man's children and his garden both reflect the amount of weeding done during the growing season.

UNKNOWN

*F*athers, like mothers, are not born. Men grow into fathers—and fathering is a very important stage in their development.

DAVID M. GOTTESMAN

*H*appy is the father whose child finds his attempts to amuse it amusing.

ROBERT LYND

—⁂—

*D*on't demand respect as a parent. Demand civility and insist on honesty. But respect is something you must earn—with kids as well as adults.

WILLIAM ATTWOOD

*M*y father is my idol, so I always did everything like him. He used to work two jobs and still come home happy every night. He didn't do drugs or drink, and he wouldn't let anyone smoke in his house. Those are rules I adopted, too.

EARVIN "MAGIC" JOHNSON

*M*y grandfather once told me that there were two kinds of people: those who do the work and those who take the credit. He told me to try to be in the first group; there was much less competition.

INDIRA GANDHI

There are some extraordinary fathers who seem, during the whole course of their lives, to be giving their children reasons for being consoled at their death.

JEAN DE LABRUYERE

—m—

I don't want to be a pal, I want to be a father.

CLIFTON FADIMAN

*I*t is admirable for a man to take his son fishing, but there is a special place in heaven for the father who takes his daughter shopping.

JOHN SINOR

—⟡—

*T*here are only two lasting bequests we can give to our children. One of these is roots, the other wings.

HODDING CARTER

*N*one of you can ever be proud enough of being the child of SUCH a Father who has not his equal in this world-so great, so good, so faultless. Try, all of you, to follow in his footsteps and don't be discouraged, for to be really in everything like him none of you, I am sure, will ever be. Try, therefore, to be like him in some points, and you will have acquired a great deal.

VICTORIA, QUEEN OF ENGLAND

*M*en are more like the times they live in than they are like their fathers.

ALI IBN-ABI-TALIB

—⟋⟋⟍—

*E*very generation revolts against its fathers and makes friends with its grandfathers.

LEWIS MUMFORD

*M*y father instilled in me the attitude of prevailing. If there's a challenge, go for it. If there's a wall to break down, break it down.

DONNY OSMOND

*H*e who is taught to live upon little owes more to his father's wisdom than he who has a great deal left him does to his father's care.

WILLIAM PENN

*I*t is impossible to please all the world and one's father.

J. DE LA FONTAINE BOOK III. FABLE 1.

—⋙—

*I*t now costs more to amuse a child than it once did to educate his father.

VAUGHN MONROE

Show me a man who has no fear and I'll show you a man who's never changed a diaper. Fatherhood is the most courageous of all occupations.

W. H. MERTZ III

—⟋⟍—

The worst misfortune that can happen to an ordinary man is to have an extraordinary father.

AUSTIN O'MALLEY

*M*y father taught me to work; he did not teach me to love it. I never did like to work, and I don't deny it. I'd rather read, tell stories, crack jokes, talk, laugh—anything but work.

ABRAHAM LINCOLN

The chances are that you will never be elected president of the country, write the great American novel, make a million dollars, stop pollution, end racial conflict, or save the world. However valid it may be to work at any of these goals, there is another one of higher priority—to be an effective parent.

LANDRUM R. BOLLING

*H*e would say sometimes, when he was in the midst of the comforts of this life, "All this, and heaven too!"

MATTHEW HENRY, ABOUT HIS FATHER

— ℳ —

*F*ew things are more satisfying than seeing your children have teenagers of their own.

DOUG LARSON

One of life's greatest mysteries is how the boy who wasn't good enough to marry your daughter can be the father of the smartest grandchild in the world.

JEWISH PROVERB

I have found the best way to give advice to your children is to find out what they want and then advise them to do it.

HARRY S. TRUMAN

—⟋⟍—

*T*he best inheritance a parent can give to his children is a few minutes of their time each day.

M. GRUNDLER

*T*o understand your parents' love you must raise children yourself.

CHINESE PROVERB

—⚬⚬—

*L*ife affords no greater responsibility, no greater privilege, than the raising of the next generation.

C. EVERETT KOOP

A grandfather was walking through his yard when he heard his granddaughter repeating the alphabet in a tone of voice that sounded like a prayer. He asked her what she was doing. The little girl explained: "I'm praying, but I can't think of exactly the right words, so I'm just saying all the letters, and God will put them together for me, because He knows what I'm thinking."

CHARLES B. VAUGHAN

There are fathers who do not love their children; there is no grandfather who does not adore his grandson.

VICTOR HUGO

—⫘—

Fatherhood is the ironman triathlon.

HUGH O'NEILL

I suppose you think that persons who are as old as your father and myself are always thinking about very grave things, but I know that we are meditating the same old themes that we did when we were ten years old, only we go more gravely about it.

HENRY DAVID THOREAU

*C*hildren today are tyrants. They contradict their parents, gobble their food, and tyrannize their teachers.

SOCRATES

—⚡—

*E*very father expects his boy to do the things he wouldn't do when he was young.

KIN HUBBARD

*N*ormally, children learn to gauge rather accurately from the tone of their parent's voice how seriously to take his threats. Of course, they sometimes misjudge and pay the penalty.

LOUIS KAPLAN

*T*here are to us no ties at all just in being a father. A son is distinctly an acquired taste. It's the practice of parenthood that makes you feel that, after all, there may be something in it.

HEYWOOD C. BROUN

*I*t is easier for a father to have children than for children to have a real father.

POPE JOHN XXIII

———❧———

A man cannot leave a better legacy to the world than a well-educated family.

THOMAS SCOTT

I talk and talk and talk, and I haven't taught people in fifty years what my father taught by example in one week.

MARIO CUOMO

*M*y father gave me the greatest gift anyone could give another person, he believed in me.

JIM VALVANO

*I*n the next year or so, my signature will appear on $60 billion of United States currency. More important to me, however, is the signature that appears on my life—the strong, proud, assertive handwriting of a loving father and mother.

KATHERINE D. ORTEGA

No music is so pleasant to my ears as that word—
father.

LYDIA M. CHILD

—⁓—

How on earth could he have slaved, denied himself,
kept going all those years without the promise
forever before him of the boy's stepping into his
shoes carrying on where he left off.

KATHERINE MANSFIELD

I felt something impossible for me to explain in words. Then when they took her away, it hit me. I got scared all over again and began to feel giddy. Then it came to me—I was a father.

NAT KING COLE

*T*rue maturity is only reached when a man realizes he has become a father figure to his girlfriends' boyfriends—and he accepts it.

LARRY MCMURTRY

—⚬—

*Y*ou can't compare me to my father. Our similarities are different.

DALE BERRA, YOGI BERRA'S SON

*A*ny man can be a father but it takes someone special to be a dad.

ANNE GEDDES

*M*y father taught me that the only way you can make good at anything is to practice, and then practice some more.

PETE ROSE

———〜〜———

A father is a man who expects his son to be as good a man as he meant to be.

FRANK A. CLARK

———
134

*T*oo bad I didn't appreciate how smart he was. I could have learned a lot from him.

UNKNOWN

—QUOTED IN ANN LANDERS COLUMN, FATHER'S DAY 1999

—⚬⚬—

*W*hen I was a boy I used to do what my father wanted. Now I have to do what my boy wants. My problem is: When am I going to do what I want?

SAM LEVENSON

*T*he thing to remember about fathers is, they're men. A girl has to keep it in mind: They are dragon-seekers, bent on improbable rescues. Scratch any father, you find someone chock-full of qualms and romantic terrors, believing change is a threat— like your first shoes with heels on, like your first bicycle it took such months to get.

PHYLLIS MCGINLEY

*T*he average man will bristle if you say his father was dishonest, but he will brag a little if he discovers that his great-grandfather was a pirate.

BERN WILLIAMS

—⦿—

*A*ny father who thinks he's all important should remind himself that this country honors fathers only one day a year while pickles get a whole week.

UNKNOWN

LEONTINE: An only son, sir, might expect more indulgence.

CROAKER: An only father, sir, might expect more obedience.

OLIVER GOLDSMITH IN *THE GOOD-NATURED MAN*

—⁂—

*A*n angry father is most cruel towards himself.

PUBLIUS SYRUS

*I*f I expect my kids to tell me what I want to know,
I need to listen to what they want to say.

ROBERT J. MORGAN

—⚉—

*M*y father gave me these hints on speech-making:
"Be sincere . . . be brief . . . be seated."

JAMES ROOSEVELT

My Daddy

When I was:

4 years old: My daddy can do anything.

5 years old: My daddy knows a whole lot.

6 years old: My dad is smarter than your dad.

8 years old: My dad doesn't know exactly everything.

10 years old: In the olden days, when my dad grew up, things were sure different.

12 years old: Oh, well, naturally, Dad doesn't know anything about that. He is too old to remember his childhood.

14 years old: Don't pay any attention to my dad. He is so old-fashioned.

21 years old: Him? My Lord, he's hopelessly out-of-date.

25 years old: Dad knows about it, but then he should, because he has been around so long.

30 years old: Maybe we should ask Dad what he thinks. After all, he's had a lot of experience.

35 years old: I'm not doing a single thing until I talk to Dad.

40 years old: I wonder how Dad would have handled it. He was so wise.

50 years old: I'd give anything if Dad were here now so I could talk this over with him.

TERI WILHELMS

What Makes A Dad?

God took the strength of a mountain,
The majesty of a tree,
The warmth of a summer sun,
The calm of a quiet sea,
The generous soul of nature,
The comforting arm of night,

The wisdom of the ages,
The power of the eagle's flight,
The joy of a morning in spring,
The faith of a mustard seed,
The patience of eternity,
The depth of a family need.
Then God combined these qualities.
When there was nothing more to add,
He knew His masterpiece was complete,
And so, He called it . . . "DAD!"

UNKNOWN